Proud Flesh

JOHN WILKINSON was born in London in 1953 and grew up in Cornwall and Devon. After a career in mental health work in Birmingham, Swansea and East London, in 2005 he joined the Keough Institute for Irish Studies, University of Notre Dame, as Poet in Residence, and teaches in the Department of English. With his wife, the literary critic Maud Ellmann, he lives between Mishawaka, IN and Cambridge, England.

DREW MILNE is the Judith E Wilson Lecturer in Drama and Poetry, Faculty of English, University of Cambridge. His books include *The Damage* (Salt, 2001) and *Go Figure* (Salt, 2003).
http://drewmilne.tripod.com

Also by John Wilkinson:

Oort's Cloud (Barque/Subpress Collective, 1999)
Effigies Against the Light (Salt, 2001)
Signs of an Intruder (Paratixis Editions, 2001)
Contrivances (Salt, 2003)
Iphigenia (Barque, 2004)

Proud Flesh

John Wilkinson

Introduction by Drew Milne

CAMBRIDGE

PUBLISHED BY SALT PUBLISHING
PO Box 937, Great Wilbraham, Cambridge PDO CB1 5JX United Kingdom
PO Box 202, Applecross, Western Australia 6153

All rights reserved

© John Wilkinson, 2005
Introduction © Drew Milne, 2005

The right of John Wilkinson to be identified as the
author of this work has been asserted by him in accordance
with Section 77 of the Copyright, Designs and Patents Act 1988.

This book is in copyright. Subject to statutory exception
and to provisions of relevant collective licensing agreements,
no reproduction of any part may take place without the written
permission of Salt Publishing.

First published by Délires and Equofinality 1986
Second edition 2005

Printed and bound in the United Kingdom by Lightning Source

Typeset in Swift 9.5 / 13

*This book is sold subject to the conditions that it shall not,
by way of trade or otherwise, be lent, re-sold, hired out,
or otherwise circulated without the publisher's prior consent
in any form of binding or cover other than that in which
it is published and without a similar condition including this
condition being imposed on the subsequent purchaser.*

ISBN-13 978 1 84471 065 2 paperback
ISBN-10 1 84471 065 3 paperback

SP

1 3 5 7 9 8 6 4 2

Contents

Acknowledgements   vii
Introduction by Drew Milne   ix

Proud Flesh   1

Index of first lines   83

Acknowledgements

Proud Flesh was published first in 1986 by Equofinality, Łodz, and Délires, Liverpool—exotic marks of origin which for Délires meant Geoff Ward and Lynette Hunter, who had published my previous book, *Clinical Notes*, and for Equofinality meant Rod Mengham, then a British Council lecturer in Poland, and my editorial collaborator in the journal of that name. All three publishers were impoverished junior academics in 1986, and put their scarce money and time into the book's appearance. I remain grateful to them.

The text of this new edition was prepared by Beric Livingstone, whose scrupulous care identified a number of errors which had escaped me.

The poems were written in Bournville, Birmingham, where I hope the house's fig tree still bears its hard fruit.

JOHN WILKINSON
CAMBRIDGE 2005

Introduction
By Drew Milne

Some of *Proud Flesh*'s initial intrigue lay in the book's physical appearance. The first edition sported a simple unglossy card cover with a colour approaching blood red: no backcover blurbs, no bar code, no notes on the author or photograph, not even stuff about the publishers. The title page identified the publishers as a mysterious compound: Equofinality out of Łodz, Poland, and Délires from Liverpool. In the mid 1980s Liverpool was associated more with militant politics than post-modern poetics. Collaboration with Poland hinted at hands across the cold war, a letter from Brezhnev with a sound track by the Gang of Four—the post-punk rockers rather than some post-Maoist cell dishing out fanzines from the ivory tower. In those long off days, when *google* wasn't yet a verb, it would have taken quite a bit of research to reveal the guiding spirits behind the book. A distribution address in Birmingham only hinted at John Wilkinson's context of production, the place where most of these poems were written.

Too much can be made of such networks, as though the underlying reality were the Cambridge nexus that forged many such connections. The confident anonymity of *Proud Flesh*'s publishers indicated that the book was the thing, not the group hug of affiliations and prize citations designed to reassure the wary. Even the epigraphs were tucked away at the back of the book, suggesting the need for a prior encounter with the text itself. This relatively austere mode of publication could have been mistaken for a late flowering of pure poetry, as if proximity to critical gossip were poison to art. More to the point, however, were the energies of independent publishing. Absence of hype suggested a post-punk resistance to commercial packaging, but also a commitment to the excitement of discovering work shorn of filters and branding, as if introductory and mediating gestures were best kept to a minimum. The distance from the protocols of academic presses and trade paperbacks indicated social hopes.

It's worth pausing over shifting publication contexts, lest historical differences collapse too quickly into false familiarity. In truth, however, the matter of the text remains the thing. Minor differences of presentation—such as 'aperatif' now altered to 'aperitif'—can be left to first edition fetishists and scholars of textual variants. More important is some recognition of this book's conceptuality as poetic sequence, as a *book* of poetry, as 'text' even, rather than as pure poetry or poetry as such. In the 1980s, before *text* became a verb associated with mobile phones, the poetics of text and textuality suggested debates exemplified by Roland Barthes' essay 'From Work to Text'.[1] Synthesizing diffuse currents, Barthes positioned 'text' as an orientation: conceiving writing as a methodological field, as a productive activity rather than as an object or finished product to be consumed. Oriented to process rather than to stable conventions or classical forms, texts develop writing as a decomposition of traditional hierarchies and genres, producing a space in which no one language has authority over any other. Despite the efforts of prose fundamentalists and latter-day prosodic traditionalists, the situation of contemporary language unsettles any tidy hierarchy of prose over poetry, or of poetry over prose.

The orientation to *text* suggested by Barthes marked one attempt to conceptualise the tendencies of avant-garde *writing* amid the ruins of traditional genres. Many of Wilkinson's contemporaries produced difficult or hermetic poems without challenging the authority of poetry as such, sometimes relying on 'Poetry' with a capital 'P' as the implicit authority motivating otherwise arbitrary collages and assemblages, as if poetry could be seized as some commanding height of meaning. Wilkinson, by contrast, has produced a series of poetic sequences which evidently engage with the traditions, languages and protocols of poetry, especially lyric poetry, but which turn such conventions against themselves. Rather than abandoning or excluding poetry in favour of a prose textuality made up of every other type of language or discourse, questions about the power of poetry continue to animate Wilkinson's texts. For those nervous of traditional poetic forms, perhaps the most alarming regularity in *Proud Flesh* is the four line stanza that figures as a shape on so many pages. *Proud Flesh* also offers challenging encounters with the gendered power relations conjured by pronouns such as 'he' and 'she', as if the reader were asked to journey into some new Baudelairean *fleurs du mal*. These, and other remnants of poetic convention, position *Proud Flesh* as a text still recognisable as a collection of poems, working through lyric process in ways akin to modernism's sceptical reworking of late romanticism. Wilkinson's writing nevertheless weaves individual 'poems' into sequences, developing a texture of poetic fragments within larger language frames and serial patterns. A sense of this orientation to writing as *text* and the associated theoretical debates, helps to specify the critical context against which *Proud Flesh* offered an unusual departure. This text, along with Wilkinson's subsequent books, emerges, accordingly, as a late modernist exploration into the limits of poetry, engaging with post-modern conceptions of writing, but reluctant to join with those for whom 'poetry' should become subject to the force of a historical taboo.

Proud Flesh might then seem to resemble a collection of poems, but this is nowhere stated in the book as such, save as an intimation of the way a diversity of texts are laid out on the page *as if* they were poems, *as if* the conventions of lineation and white space might still be read as poetic conventions. Each page can be read either as a singular poem or as text, either as an example of poetry or as part of a field of textuality constructed by this book. Something similar is true of the status of what might be construed as representations of subjective experience in *Proud Flesh*. It is hard not to read a number of pages as poems articulating experiential reflections—memories, dreams, fantasies, desires, pillow talk—reflections, it might be inferred, upon an ongoing but private sub-text. As a sequence of poems and as text, *Proud Flesh* nevertheless makes it possible to perceive this language of experience as a series of social frames, as social and aesthetic discourses mediating and enabling experience, in short as experiences *of* language rather than experiences *in* language. As well as being overdetermined by the framing of experience as 'poetry'—what would love between two people be if it had no poetry?—the mediation of impulses as lyric impulses also inhibits, prevents, falsifies even, the very types of experience lyric traditionally seeks to represent. Reading each page as a lyric fragment nevertheless brings the reader up against frames which suggest family resemblances and associations shared by different pages and across the book as a 'whole'. Sustained reading of the whole nevertheless cannot quite take the book as a 'whole', cannot quite find a coherent structure or system of meaning. Shared cadences and pulses become recognizable, along with overlapping clusters and diffuse discursive modes. But the idea that there might be some conceptual structure or paradigm articulating the book as a whole reveals itself as a fantasy, no more or less plausible than a variety of other ways of coping or responding, including the desire to control meaning or language. Read as *text*, the book evades interpretation according to an architectonic, conceptual or procedural core, remaining provisional, differential and improvised. This internal differentiation and resistance to system nevertheless involves deliberation amid competing determinations, a dance of the intellect which is more than accidental or the result of some arbitrary rule. Each page or poem is not an instance of some underlying conceptual or cognitive paradigm, such as phenomenology or psychoanalysis, but one among a series of texts whose differences from each other determine the book's textual space.

Proud Flesh develops its own textual arena, then, both close to the limits of poetry as an orientation to meaning and yet sceptical of heroic conceptual paradigms that seek to subsume poetry within some other hierarchy of meaning or cognition. This orientation to text and textuality helps to illuminate the awkward status of 'lyric' in *Proud Flesh*. Introducing a recent anthology of contemporary poetry in which Wilkinson's work is featured, Rod Mengham argues that what binds together the anthology's 'various kinds of innovative practice is a strong insistence on finding ways of continuing and renewing the lyric impulse in poetry in English'.[2] A number of poets in the anthology would query this characterisation, but Wilkinson's texts bring the problem into sharp relief, appearing both to affirm and to undermine the centrality of lyric impulses. Understood as sequential texts, as collected fragments of a larger texture which does not cohere into an organic or singular work, Wilkinson's procedures foreground both the desire for lyric affirmation and a necessary unsettling of the face values associated with lyric. Citing John Wieners as a precedent, Wilkinson himself has suggested in an interview that: 'the words from the lyric are something so compromised or so difficult to simply accept, at the very moment of lyric impulse there is also a negation of that, and to that extent I feel that almost everything I do is a sort of failed love poem.'[3] This emphasis on negation and failure marks out a very different conception of writing from the self-preening associated with affirmative, achieved work or, perhaps more critically, from the supposedly humble tone of tentatively tremulous sensitivity which still passes for poetic perception in some circles. Wilkinson's sequences have a characteristic generosity and dynamic extension but with a no less energetic capacity to deflate and deflect. This negation of lyric impulse is not a procedural negativity, however, working through irony or satire, but a lack of composure, a discomfort within the energy of composition:

> *Proud Flesh* more than any other of my extended works represents an attempt to write a love poem, a short love poem. And it represents a repeated and I hope interesting failure to do so. It tackles centrally the question of relative power in an erotic relationship, or in an erotic need. It questions erotic need at the very moment that it arises, and at the moment that it would govern the making of the text. It is uncomfortable with the projections into the loved one which are the basis of the erotic need. It's uncomfortable with the colonization of the loved one by those projections. This is the central material of the text. The loved one in *Proud Flesh* is white, is marble, is ice, is a place which is animated by the lover; who himself is white, marble and ice and animated by the loved one. It's full of mirrors.[4]

Such retrospective authorial reflections ought to be taken with pinches of salt, but notice the tension here between the projections of love lyric and the materiality of *text*. The exploration of love, power and lyric in *Proud Flesh* is as much concerned to negate the lyric impulse as with any attempt to renew or reaffirm the love lyric.

The quality of negation in *Proud Flesh* develops differentially, rather than dialectically. David Trotter's early characterization of John Wilkinson's writing, republished in *The L=A=N=G=U=A=G=E Book*, contrasts Wilkinson's writing with 'dialectical lyric':

> Dialectical lyric stages the drama of the 'advertising mind', in Shelley's phrase, the mind turned toward a 'vastness' which reveals itself as a lack: disenfranchised, internally riven ... The lyric voice dialectically opposed to the unsayable, discovers itself as a lack ... The texts of Mengham and Wilkinson ... are not predicated upon any such absenting moment (the generation of antithesis *out of* thesis) but rather upon the multiple infliction of one thesis on another, *different* thesis. ... We have entered a Nietzschean world where forces don't enter into relation with opposites they themselves have generated, but with other forces ...[5]

There's something uncomfortable with anything so blunt as the making of a thesis in *Proud Flesh*. The text is nevertheless strewn with assertions, exclamations and rhetorical questions that could be mistaken for programmatic propositions if abstracted from the play of forces at work in the book, as if the presiding spirit were some latter-day Nietzschean like the Gilles Deleuze of *Anti-Oedipus*.[6] Lines such as: 'Sentiments are reasons / through our flesh, they sport over the synapse & we move ...' (p. 12) make explicit strains of argument in the texture, notably the way 'flesh' is animated by desires, images and language, but this is a textual synapsis which conflates any stable condition of analogy. One of the most arresting opening lines seems to invite a reading of the text as a literary exploration of psychoanalytic object relations theory, but subsequent lines deflate the pretensions of such rhetoric, refocussing attention on poetic grammars: 'O where is the breast I left part of my mouth on? / Where did I leave off? & when you decipher me / will you find a nothing's opposite, a mere lump / or tease a catch-all cradle from my fine twist? // No-one holds to categories. The one threatening was / the one who did, the one who faked, found / truth at the end of a false trail. The character / & the nullity both bleed with unfinished business' (p. 50). Unfinished and incomplete, this is negation as difference, a reanimation of dead categories and dead metaphors, which ebbs and flows rather than becoming newly determinate.

A key juxtaposition is the mutation of the language of poetic sentiment through the quasi-scientific language of biology and brain chemistry: 'A longitudinal slice of the brain / will show two lovers fade in porcelain light to chinoiserie / that as false origin indurates' (p. 59), or 'Eyes pitched up to the dura mater. Since you were loved, so / you gain advantage. Will shrivels as tardive dyskinesia' (p. 61). Most readers will need a dictionary to follow some of the semantic loops involved. Wilkinson's work engages an exceptionally wide-ranging lexicon, but this engagement also invokes a developed scepticism for the ambiguities revealed by definitions. This much is clear from the epigraph from the *Shorter Oxford English Dictionary*, which appears to locate the semantic field of the book's title in relation to clinical or medical language, as if the texts that make up the book were growths built on or around healing wounds. Medical language is one of the resources explored in the book, but the text of *Proud Flesh* exceeds such definition, suggesting a poetics of metaphor and analogy, one much animated by the resources of adjectival compounds, from 'unshockable plasm' or 'cool romance' to 'lax spring' and 'reckless salvo'. Recklessly transgressing Poundian and objectivist injunctions against such uses of the adjective, the resulting compounds become unnervingly productive nodes of meaning, transitional turns in which discourses crash and splinter. One word put under particular strain by this text is 'like'. Simile after simile puts pressure on the powers of analogy-making, but this staple of lyric enlargement becomes a suspiciously promiscuous projection: 'She assimilates all comparison into her like ... // from clouds of *so like her* ... // ... these our pranks /

frequent her like witnesses, o intense inane / they jostle, even the stars are like stops / that shearing a torso out of fierce love // colonize its phantom limbs to prove her body' (p. 77). The troubling ratio of living beings to idealised or aestheticised figures, alluded to in the other concluding epigraph, undermines the desire for similes rather than affirming the evident fecundity with which this writing produces similes: 'Can this be how we inflate // our meaning presence from our demeaned lives / caressing the part-payments?' (p. 75) Counting the cost of the lyric impulse generates a text whose interest is the reverse of the inflated poetics of achievement. Among the many pleasures afforded by this differential text are its glimpses of freedom from the lyrical poetics of love.

1 Roland Barthes, 'From Work to Text', *Image / Music / Text*, ed. & trans. by Stephen Heath (London: Fontana, 1977), pp. 155-164.

2 Rod Mengham, 'Introduction', *Vanishing Points: New Modernist Poems*, eds. John Kinsella and Rod Mengham (Cambridge: Salt, 2004), pp. xvii-xix (p. xix).

3 'The John Wilkinson Interview', *Angel Exhaust* 8 (1992), 76-90 (79).

4 'The John Wilkinson Interview, part 2', *Angel Exhaust* 9 (1993), 69-77 (70).

5 David Trotter, 'Voices-Off: Mengham and Wilkinson', *The L=A=N=G=U=A=G=E Book*, eds. Bruce Andrews and Charles Bernstein (Carbondale and Edwardsville: Southern Illinois University Press, 1984), pp. 251-3 (pp. 251-2).

6 Cf. Gilles Deleuze and Félix Guattari, *Anti-Oedipus: Capitalism and Schizophrenia*, trans. R. Hurley, M. Seem and H.R. Lane (Minneapolis, Minnesota, 1983).

Proud Flesh

Slender pickings fall to the lap of the foster-child
who chides them into their own spheres, the nuclei
of unshockable plasm, home like everything he touches
will be compèred by the memories they create before

dust settles, spawn begins to heave. Is he socially
acceptable? Does he use a knife & fork with facility?
Will he boil his underwear, when living in the world
where prompts are few? Do you rate his speech lucid?

does he spill his life-blood over a phrase, & refuse
to clear up? The quills he flurries from his spine
thread these poor facts of life, draw them out & turn
the loops separately to tap his fluid. Any capsule

of love, any midnight pearl, has had him for a unique
sponsor to its quality, concocting in his parietal
lobe a cool romance. There, for this gaunt clarity
its positive was pressed to a dilapidated back-yard

They bash their fists on the asphalt playground, as if
they could crush the stone below; soft fists splinter
A) ache, B) pale white secure, C) deep white safeline
Sparks from the mica fan into veins, & tar-thick milk

shrouds the quartz, jade, or plumps that rose-quartz
hollow under its bitumen teat. We turn through shades
but click in the small white statue smelling of milk
with human dirt, with a sweet taint. O my boat, beat

downstream in the tunnel, your pennants & gypsy décor
nosing the sedge already for cute traces of light; ray
out as emerging you leave your heart behind. Children
beat this vault with their fists, & their fists bleed

Every metaphor sounds the same
in its sepia, dry blood melancholy

but if you cry, it drips blood
onto the quarry tiles

so you hasten for the authentic
rasp of the next & the next

leaving behind you dying homunculae

Clay when the wire slackens, sheds its velvet light
self-contained. No secret gleams out of the cleft
You take off an outside, make something of it. Take
the next outside, turn it too for the light's vessel

All the gang of your dreams rises out of the crease
you've lit, fanning with fruit beside the escalier
loaded with green pods of flesh. Your scooped shells
lie scattered & whitening, lime for the tree-roots

Your griefs will have worked the beautiful trellises
that fig has scaled; & a swag of fruit, the alien
pelf will be plumped in intimate gifts at your feet
Clay pods, they swell in your dreams' commissariat

bulging out like a thumb; or in a civic statuary made
lush as the poor transfigured lives are fed to the
moloch of sleepy entanglement. Time they shall stick
for any respite, from time that knackers the flesh

splitting off over the dunes, in the cupped light
they quaff & by which they pay homage. Their figtree
staggers with leaden fruit, & the almond chokes up
floss. Outside are these witnesses to your fashion

We'd launch out, but a spiral failure binds so close
our dwindling inner city. Moths form their tiny scrip
with charred wings, flock the arena though we twist
a loop from their royal flight; fatty it too with coils

scarred indelibly now drops through lipid space; what
vertical links, agents, forwarding or poste restante
can ever again grip the headstalk! With every reason
moths subdue the heart, reinforce its white bulwark

swift as a bat to sound our ugly orphans, to flush
the always-dear. They screw the head for kaleidoscope
how our dreams squawk! No choice but stand to reason
soon as look at a festered heart there's no two ways

but pitfall in a dead-stick-loop, but the backfire
from tongues which churn our spectra, which speculate
our sightedness; no, such canutes flesh the dry flesh
like a can of figs. Past help, & all saving. Reason

shuts the window tight & grouts the wall with cilia
mapping our neural paths; that moon we stir to launch
will only sail as transom for a moss-scented flush
of white peaks, rooftops, leaching the stooped pylon

He smears
fresh shit on his hands

he holds
them up with his arms

O fleece them
with blonde hair

thick as trowel, honky
ice

Doors open to the metal crash of insects, & outside
the first stain of lichen bulks on blotting-paper
Capercailzie shriek. A buzz-saw coughs. Men pull
off, in hoof-prints they leave behind them. Hounds

chew their hide loops & totter about the shithouse:
All pain is deliberate, or it will be if it isn't
tractable to daddy's smirch, watch it in the mirror
Self-absorbed we might be, yet cruelly given over

to those micro-organisms swimming through our eyes
My face is what I see. You grind me for a choice
of if to grind me. You should, you might have done
within your rights. But the musculature degenerates

cells disperse to every joint & reach the brain
The outside world convulses like a coseismic web
It's 'non-organ-specific'. Rivers start to appear
& elms to creak. Kine appear to fall at their knees

In the losing light, see, your head
tilts to a cold frame outside
filled with refuse. There the rusty
maiden turns unadorned, & creaks
fearfully at the verge of stupor

Shifts of light fail, but one near
command of wind can cause her
still to vary, unselfconscious
out cold. So the one or other
left & right, you and she descant

holding, as the dusk a birdcall
sustains, a gleam, one component
saved from an intense group
You, the wanted understanding
sap the kaolin heaps, tighten grass

while you perfect your half-face
& see, white water's fret disturbs
lively mud, throwing glances
like a retrospective crystal. As I
will be, I had every cause to think

I was. But she grinds in her condyl
all that's known by heart
cloaks the tongue your counter-
poise would furl back. She refers
foreign calls to her program

planting a likeness in plain air
cricking the field's neck
to evade you. Ill-matched couples
spit, & a cone, a pine gland
burns next to this silent area

Vision clots to a pearl. Denoted
at a loose end, we face each other
riding roughshod over the fugue
of steps to come. Pearl's intent
goes native, more than likely

analogue of its last fling
& the usual quota of small fish
sings so floridly in its rut
had better talk. For kaolin forms
its purpose, what it faces

thinks attractive thought
to its purpose, faulting a shadow
what in no space inheres, only
caught like a metal ghost on
light-sensitive grass, its gleam

counts, matters. Clay that's host
to the light it stuns, old
shut-eye, heart is a lump
dilates no longer; now it is cool
with its quartz hum

now shrill & electrostatic. Heart
shrinks, & over that tread
the sulphur flowers bud anticly
We scent the diastole
of our loose beginning. Gorse

flowers rotate, but never bloom
a yellow piecemeal
on the damp habitual, uninhabited
beat of the heart. Hold us in view
submissive & outright titled

Where light slashes I'll break into flower. Does brocade
of lillies, light congealed, best parry a stooge's pass
or will the bloody stigma stay? Sentiments are reasons
through our flesh, they sport over the synapse & we move

A hit, a clot can alter our kinship at gut-level, & warp
the hand's riposte. Is the plume picked off or entirely
bidden by solar vents, teased by a puff of scant air?
Shall we rotate so fast as to all intents be motionless?

Pavements I walk
have rheum laid on with a trowel

& morning
plastered with rime & sleep

begins to cake on my eyes
I am in the place of equivalence

as a trained observer, I am
up to my neck

& must this heart too roam
till it is fatty & solid also?

But ours is another ploy for power amidst blueberry hills
Your mouth hard as a shrub bruises sky until that blue
Deceptively our shadows lengthen till their loaded claws
bite the mutant chromosome. It does, they do that well

& her eye bulges now as a kidney does in its lard purse
unwrenchable by cue or affect; even a crack to get shot
of this whole thing, benighted every so hotly doesn't blow
the staunch loop. If a blue moth clips, clips her proud

flesh to soft-cell comeback, to a red echo, & that side-
issue wants its innate source, though dominant light fall
in massive chunks, breaks them up who doused in tallow
stick to their sunny nervous path, well what do you know

complementary, out of hand, plunges into your spinal itch
cut where the senses-off make sense of a distant column
Their raw mauve hardly shifts. That is as may be will be
blaze the recessive gene for she in my brain's body-bits

Geomancers pick among these trinkets in their play-pen
tweezing inlaid pearls, setting rubies so their flush
will thud into a maisonette where women have set to
to shine their instruments; to scour the free marks off

scattering them on glass dishes, screw them in her eye
like motes that grow enveloped in the white of white
The flaw wherewith I speak shall rub them out totally
Malfunction deep in prime space, the hope I've dithered

tracks her with regret whose only self, the sand coupé
frisks outlying phantom legs, spread to await a surge
minutes before the lamp goes white at intersections
What does the earth foresee, straining colour? My heart

sinks, my face drops, you'll lose your head, this hand
in its blobby medium, fate sealed in a special ring's
pigeon-blood. Its red sea anaemone shrinks to the rock
Beads of sperm go hard on the pearly lid of a jewel-box

Darkness, thickly feathered, squats to eat, the lucid
inch across their evidence, like the stars engrave
a fixed lens. No despair, doubt or joy shall induce
eclipsed blood to meekly rise, yet its bulb can burst

& heart's confusion stain remembered loops, misshape
the radishes that whiten cerebrally, could overlap
her overlapping tenuous thoughts. The frail brig is
caulked with sexual pain. A forest hut, tannery floor

bleeding now from dead space; when lips are bruised
from tender shock, the sick blue leather smell causes
little fist to pulse, she branchless can't inhibit
Yield to meet her in that depth her memories appoint

by their dissembly; you could die of self-sufficience
if you won't fall from empathy. At the astronomer's
least whim, blades of grass cut each way both shares
overt in a nursery colour candle's shake and gutter

A fat photograph
about to be cropped

where what is incidental
bloats an incident

with light or dead space
The elements

will say *Ah*
drawn close

the moles & needles
drill unpractised flesh

She dies less
for points of their

invention, solid caps
over points of entry

than a quick-to-the-jaw
reasonableness

without waste or
overlapping

idly ripping
incidental blossom off

X marks your hinterness
with a foxed stare

where love crushes
silver backs to splinters

& looking glass goes clear

Moths feed at this window, bury their drear heads in light
At the end of a stammer of false moves I stall with love
for a freckled neck, for a freckled ripe plum. & on I limp
to the view I semble out from plaster, putty, resin & acid

poured in a cone of scarred canvas. Moths then do a round
tapping their invoices, promptly given the world outside
within as a cyclorama. Moths tap for the least window tax
like a sugar advent turning nasty. Open that mouth of yours

Your words catch in the throat that I gulp & incessantly
bring them up & you say, you remember that! but I don't
recede with my wistful cup. For sheer neck you would take
like a sharp white fold again as you stretch, your vigil

always to take out more, disdains their moth made flesh
bobbing like Adam's apple. This stone lodged in my gullet
I shall esteem as bread. You lift my voice & it dilatory
flutters, moth to a throat. Shut your trap on my say-so

The key that fastens the door turns any lock in my body
over its grooves, splitting the cylinder out into leaves
like a chestnut buds as a paralysed polyp exquisitely
racked on the empyrean, twists those nipples which ooze

neuroconductors, ripping their down of appeasement off
Mink & waterrats burrow more tiers, an unruffled surface
breaks to small festoons; the clay ridge running beside
pierced with boltholes, filigree young nettles pierce

like joints the fistful lashes behind the shed, when in
dirt one quiet & grateful, rises to embrace its sphynx
Loops lie on the brick earth floor unplayed & indistinct
The opposite lock floods in oil but squeaks compatibly

Cloud-blue affliction skims & trails his antibodies
off a defiled civic crust, the wych-elm is abandoned
to device. Untalented, his voice's solid ghost does
not interpret, nor can it thieve the instinctive act

when draining a cup he shows his gentle knife, when
eating with one another he taps, that cruet to hand
will chasten wicks' intent free fire; if klieg lamps
soothe his furious shade, he twirls the radioactive

eyepencil, gladly scumbles death in freaks of memory
to a solemn dawn-effect. O concentrate their new *dot*
of life corrupt the foetal bonds; their parallels
streak yellowly to wax the beehive retina, & cramped

bleary, predatory rash in greed of substance, braced
on work rails they sweat & drizzle & mist, reenact
fight/flight response where motor nerves had crimped
the signal:—shall death drench their whitish strip

through & thoroughly? can one short its electric run
of meals? shoot over its chiasm? launch an impulse?
dab with the pre-oil saved from hope his miniatures
that weepingly succumb to direct order? Shove it, do

not call an emergent voice to book. But let it shake
in the gourmet airstream, as in a heliograph the sun
précises to one period. This could be no predictable
cycle or voice, but gently qualified, gently steers

Lorraine will cruise
tail-lights on the blink

above you, listening
like an amphitheatre

to your tottering
on the metal studs

scoring tries
with pencil marks

on the dead white
banisters, her knees skid

work to quicklime
to a crease

Or is it Crab-boy
raps the alien twig

one hand free
for wringing himself

jerks in a turret
bird's-neck beady eye

Maybe a chicken-choker
lensman

for Nazi
chess-sets & bone

philosophy doctors
gone occult & leather, fist

fucked by immanent will
& photographed

with bleeding elbow
sticking from his arse

The gear-shift lever
sticks, the motive

crooks the dog's-leg
gate we squeeze round

in a barbican
of tiered cake & shit

Breaker one-nine
Breaker one-nine

Nicky here in the armed camp
the old pike

the military road where steel
tracks strike off flints

& their yolks
smell of fire & decaying
mushrooms, soaking down
through pine needles

but recoil, as if that mat
were a trampoline

Will the man in the moon blink in his stuffy globe?
will he transgress, or pinpoint, or cause crows
or car transporters, song-thrushes, does he fidget
now against the earth, squeaking as if in a balloon?

                              —If any blinks
his body's a corpse from then in its given sphere

& begins to chatter at once. Immediately it squirms
to read itself, a flypaper running after its coils

As flickerbooks of the blistered but perennial ice
creep the well-loved characters, craning out of
shadows which now parcel out his shadow's backform
for others engineering space; they get in a flap

deliberately to help their balance, their ascetic
arms retense along the tendons to meet the strain
of white eyes, whose passage herds without a blink
their sharp reflexiveness; no degrading eyelight

escapes to sully the belt so swift that it won't
turn on any account. So statues slip off the wall
& skate & doodle over the ice, chickens whom death
preens in a cool display of powderroom attitudes

taking them off, transferring them into travesties
till only death can force, only death construes
these dummies about the margin, their blank eyes
taunted in tunnel vision. It won't intimidate him

bandied with liberty through the ends & attitudes
held for his flesh as a camera to develop at once
or even before; the flash of his disenchantment
gels their dreams to a thick skin, quashes touch

Does snow or polystyrene, crisp the noise he went after
shrink so early, squat as a hindu god on palsied grass?
Such travesties now clamour aloud to have each sense
rescheduled to the stem; shadows to get their own back

in blazing offshoots, whose recanted good senses duck
beneath the rink, but leave above a backform his size
to pace a charred room, perform his ritual as allowance
He's outstripped you to the altogether, hordes of sexy

brainchildren, fleshing out the profile he's vacated
frolicking over the corpse his mouth once loved to lick
You seraphs need hands. These were his sticky thimbles
stuck in a resin tide, should've held you by the scruff

Love is brought to fulfilment by this art, distributed
through space. Shines beneath their stubbed & bare
skates, the granular forgetfulness of the neurones
Ahead of morning the white brute bends to feast there

It tears its entirety into the entity on whose spoor
their body was laid, no more to compress in the frugal
measure. But dying to handsomeness. Even a tasselled
penis skin, & her pendulous vulva neck smooth out

& the crouched neck will dribble its comb earthwards
What cruder marks can they miss? who linger to watch
white steal through colour; did his preposterous hands
die into elegance? With the winds light & variable

may a confident heart charge the sky, or its entrails
weigh off; strewn locally on a group so perfect now
float like cotton pickings? Aerodynamically astute
they beam up, still figuring whilst their figures bite

Chaff or husk or bran the dark has held fritters away
condensing that its winnower unclasps. She contemplates
mouth to yell, birds fly out to squat on the boughs
bearing each one note of this, her cant. She is marble

stele under the choking cloud-nest that the itinerant
weave her. Shout then to recant from shouting. Yell now
till the yell fillips across her face. Its frequencies
are smattering on lips they force back into a block

She is her elsewhere, cantilever, sending her distant
touch to the device, tortured fondly, straight as fancy
where the groove invites. How could she let it drop, &
race into its zig-zag over the polished, severe facet

Round her old buffoons gather pleats into their faces
shake maracas, clatter bells, court & dance, slap the
cheap guitars. None disconcerts the rank of silence
Or ruffles a countenance that nor reflects nor contains

nor shall be organised when they candy the moon's light
as off her breast, snaring in their dormer-perspective
her heart with nets of song. O savage friends, beyond
whose spry monotony her silence scatters & soars up

        Underfoot
is concentrated, birdsong so intense
          it goes unperceived, a transparent
             roar drowns it out

          Geysers throw up stars & aeroplanes
          Trees leak from mineral veins

            Hyperion to a Satyr!
        The trunk no infant can do without!
   A Seraph
       blushing through his clenched teeth!
A typical pander in Gethsemane, a crocus
   splitting his bulb on a mat of needles!
     Those seraphs *need* teeth!
They do not have six wings, the air
   has their six wings to beat them with!
                   O spiteful!
      It's like a board at your back
          covered with flinch scribbles

Waste breath drifts. Breath condenses
in the grizzled air, before a first
tumour makes shift from mud
indicting in one flaw, its bloodline
Ice pares the mountain slope

the brood of presage his contemporary
will raise, still reechoes
What should his resolve be?
Volcanic mud to nurse
a grievance, sordes to encrust his

slack lips, humor that his crystal
would dispense as balm
if at your contrary, eager stress
were light perilous (I only dream)
When sweat-faded, blanket promiscuity

wafts over the figurines to cure them
ranked before the ditch
a clay pulp, a burnt
& bready warmth, no profile flashes
fleshes out, anneals the ice crease

stiff from earth's derided throw-offs
engine-wheels & hearts shaped
to drag to mire their pain. Take
heart from that mortuary
then jump into the narrow breach

of consciousness will split your face
like a flawed crystal, gripe
the mud can cake
on hard lips; who catching breath
conversely, was each his own ancestor

Dormant flies stagger. Fleas pick holes
in a threadbare cartilage, fibres
itch the would-be speaker
Open his trap, it's wadded, a keen
north-easterly scythes the tiles

where he fantasizes below the eaves
one foot through the laths
I held my furious torch at arm's-length
bones like fish-bones in spun glass
The strands recurvate

what I would coil from, shield
my threadbare heart; the dull filaments
move to incorpse me into their reel
Greetings, welcome, old souteneur
turned on autonomous pilot

death. I'm in your midst, a cave-
dweller who dumb & short on etiquette
is spoken before he speaks
stammeringly through lips of the subject
tribe; an infidel, a helot

a *dh*immi forbidden to breathe
mortality into the words of the book;
an asthmatic, an onion-seller, a Brummie
woman who shall not mock
the faithful with her fluency—

may she not in her gutturals, name
the nameless, not mistake & tumble
seams, splitting the veil
off emptiness! Nor tug this sash
that insulates me from the clever earth!

Love compels me to its dialect, love whose law
        furs the imperial tongue

The faithful hear me at their backs & curse
        glassily

        Yes when days
were dappled as old movie-stock
I took place in the idiom of the objects'
     besetting pearls
dreamy silt over a high moor
        whispered, transubstantial

A curtain thinks in its crease
A tree thinks in its sap
              & she considers
     the sense left to a corridor
unsteadying rockpools
        surface now opaquely. I pick
through heather aghast with sleep
     where pearls glow
              & the flesh
     goes out
to love what's lost & sealed, was hollowed
        or erupts
The pearls sap & gather a strength
              flesh
     draws from the copula

Away from scavengers who scuff & pry the weary peat
a soft verdule curls up; their evidence was machined
coldly in the flats of the eye, a millionaire lens
whose curve drinks thirstily of the dew, innocent

of snap resuscitation in tufted grass, of the beads
rattling on its surface from planets where they thaw
Larvae burn for their increase. One trivial slipup
in declension rages in the polyp, & a buried seed

swells against the ulna, gathers pain of due season
How blind the air is! like candlewax. Dishevelled in
the solvents of Fort Dunlop, I feel the lump in my
throat, it's neoplasm, period to fast living, bar

anything we see is what we sow, a slip in register
off a slick jelly, a mutation in the feature; larvae
stir under the sheep-runs we rake across our dead
reckoning. Their speed in our throats now full stop

For years this had been a waking hurt. Dear violence
frosts the mouth, curved beaks yammer my flesh & cry
as if a machine gone mental, should it engage birth
thought in iron, remembers it still for pine & semen

White eyes will scribble the dark, & a faint message
blots on the starveling, glowers on coal-bright skin
starting them out, but fledge. Feast on their cones
in eyes reminiscent of cut steel. Don't let the dark

close into daylight thin as a stray mosquito, admit
this miserable pillage of birds. O thickly-feathered
darkness, eat the lucidities, flock with our dreams
from that presence to where we shall shriek in amity

Distraught with its self-aggrandisement, the brain-
children, snatch a tryst of love from its sour truth
It pours out grey sky, uproots the spitting pylons
slashes across her plump wrist a star-soaked field

What axe did the god grind, what bone could it have
to pick with her; what glum tautology, self-evident
has mapped her with its cellophane rash, its bloat
sealing her frontiers—how can she strike opaquely

that autocrat of tight lips, who found no symptoms
but is making her a memory out of members present?
Nothing to see but stale mist, a mist losing heart
close to ground, that had lost heart in the cirrus

nothing to tap but a pod of blood, as visible trauma
signs away a last cell; why should the leaves drop
on earth? It's spring if you want in the here & now
if dwelling on points to ground love or condense her

Strip the caul from my face, fold it & bury it fast
that in my avow it not supplant me. Earth do drink
a swollen pouch out of its conceit; & the voracious
solvent of our dreams, the dissolute nitty-gritty

do you consume which is all the being any affects
Their flights of fantasy get a desert into the bag
the stars, vasty deep. Under a mantelpiece my heart
horns pinch; & still born I drown in amniotic fluid

Jealously given a cup, filled with a black aperitif
streaking & plastering down his plush. Only a scare
in a batch of tins can restitute the old shambles'
blood in this glare of sacrifice. A babe in the snow

drinks at last, no-one flies though he wails & gags
I was eating myself from the great dust. I conceived
well the indolent prophet would snore, dead to my
effort of life. I broke out all over in sticky buds

Snap out of it then! Pull yourself together at once!
No I don't mean that. I mean, let go of yourself
towards me, in peril of smashing to bits with lust
Why do my looks fall off you like black confetti?

Where did you pick those up? I mean, those looks
that flit off you like backing silver? If I complete
my trust in you, can you help but break the trust
in you in myself? You needn't break but it's broken

trust shall answer for unmet lust. Meets you halfway
bodily, shall speak for you from what you bespeak
off the clear & behaved men, you're the watering
on their mirror. Or does their wafer, nil by mouth

mouth the final bereavement of you of yourself? Not
in your mouth it doesn't, the skin has been plighted
inwardly. O not on your life, when typical jerks
dissolved your image, that was a pretty compliment

was a real cinch to get you off, a fabulous stroke
uncreaturing you, bickering you like a quickstep
Shiva whom they model, shape: aren't we appropriate!
Which arms held your elbows, why do your arms whirl

dust & ashes? Gropers round you, lamia of compassion
intimate with the glass they flesh, with the flesh
glassed where thick mud has been smirched across
& the glass that struggles to cover itself reflects

I pulled it out of my lungs
with sturdy rope

I polished the toecap
wearing myself

brightly pitted & cinderous

Ice & dead skin
blister the city pavements

O make life
opposite to death again

In this trial run for behaviour, sculling then as now, a dry run
before their backlash lurches them to a leisure creek, the glass
whose roof the waves form, no-one is supervised or fears to tread
or is it as is as ever they scull on the frozen evicted shadows?

Where is the candle you turn towards away from what is all over?
Worlds of shaping power, a fortress, a great flood now inundates
the night-light, the float of a childish bed, that drift covered
with thought's very forms, are an emptiness; that tried to evict

evacuate, to total themselves like coupons at a redemption point
trawl & burn the water fished to isinglass already, glass floats
conceitedly detached heave & then beach sky's drift-net in amber
pegging out, pegging amber sands out as her topology, eflowered

Contracts
that lop-side, side-

wind amidst
the scooped tubs

of fat, nurse
doubts to pride

via the slewed gate
revisiting

a corrugated
ash sheet

they bury
snouts till transparent

This
a falange convoy

where Nicky's tired
eye rolls down a gun

emplacement, down
a tissue

of oedemic lies
revolves

till outspread
to luminescent

consoles, & the Game
Theory section

Up you get!
This

this is the big
dipper's

dead addicted
star chariot

this is the iron
limb that scrapes

bumptious horses
on the emery sky

this is
pulling off

to light shafted
into showerrooms

this
this is South

Africa, this is
Coca-Israel West Bank

frosted
aromatic sage

thrift
in red warning light

decorate
my Pimms Cup

squirt a shot
of SASOL

through the sugar
side-suckers

this is wireless
Can you move one up?

But rolling
down my stalactite

heat-pressed
in bone

my purloined
stutter paws

dendrous mud
to red marrow

osteoblasts

Nurselings of a pitched eye visit the grey stalk
& shove their surgical barbs in till stamens hinge
Whatever they want was traded back, their will
o'the wisp diffuses like mouth's oil in rivulets

shuffles up to dawn's hurt palisade. One flutter
on the past, my heart only sought whom & seeks
touching me might form me still with love. One far
too previous to lend colour to day's steel glints

true-to-form for counterfeit with a secret die
from night's stock, o weigh the twitching gauzes
of my body, its creatured mist beyond the pale. No
but ditch on a street disgraceful for cool drops

dash to the kerb its heat-haze, unstop this rain-
bow proscenium; as amber slugs can get a skinful
beyond the jealous arch, so can pink worms disport
themselves on the happy pavement by dawn's fence

Deceitful as the first breach in the sense-world
my pale duenna, my cynosure. For the aftertaste
of reproduction, *in vitro* or high fidelity, still
hangs like smoke until I wrap myself in its veil

In white gatherings of the dream, my drowned face
turns out to orient to the morning star. & she
will glance at its surface so at a second breach
my face must drown its fond totem. So to speak

orotund out of a sphere. In that sound she sleeps
like a statue, under the handsome bullet plough
insists with her silver line. The subject falls
on his 4 feet, wrings his hands, wrings his hands

How shall you dream me now I cannot devise you?
How shall you speak me now I can't pause once?
At my last gasp I want your mouth something awful
Rip the veil from solid things & choose that veil

& every soul forgive me, for I am self-forgiving
The heart lambasts its cavity & kicks at traces
as in his ideal home a paraplegic whose steel gear
frames him to the accordances of an ideal body

Whose sheeted rooms are burgled systematically
by the poor brutal children, who on his outskirts
thieve mementoes, such with the dawn's first blush
prevent him weeping with his contrivances below

the bedclothes; it is the fierce cries of siskins
perforate his ears & bend double again the sharp
despairs of love that reawaken nightly, & self
regard through the morning shroud of flesh-colours

shrieking give me give me, seizing at heavy drapes
for the morsel world; hammering that insistently
at his rib-cage, shredding through billow lace
till he forgives me as if it were his to forgive

O where is the breast I left part of my mouth on?
Where did I leave off? & when you decipher me
will you find a nothing's opposite, a mere lump
or tease a catch-all cradle from my fine twist?

No-one holds to categories. The one threatening
was the one who did, the one who faked, found
truth at the end of a false trail. The character
& the nullity both bleed with unfinished business

You put your head on the rails to hear the spot
You lift your head to the stars to switch track
Sadness shakes you through the ear you submit
to its ebbing voice, & the stars are too constant

A party's in full swing at the end of this line
but no voice talks to you in the foreground. This
is the old connection but with lips torn away
their huge head sunk on the chest in infant pain

Narrowly in the kitchen, coffee brews
in clumsy hands on an early shift
        shadowless
our open pores & pimples, press
the pane of light which slapped first
before we knew how our qualities lay
        like a tanned hide

Tumid dust is laid by the strip lamps
        Saturated hearts lie dumb & blae
with shadows, ghosts of desire
narrow their lumens & close the supply
        LVF supervenes
If we feel sympathy here
        we shall burst

So our faces swell for comparison
        But since we find none, o
let me take it all back
        folding the chain of awnings
let me replace them in their compartment
        lest with a tug
of pain we suddenly know
        phantoms lost that rove

Ghosts walk through you as much by day
had never spoken so eloquently
until once lost, finding themselves
past compare. One of these residues
gaunt twigs which snap
like charcoal skinnily wrapped in person
   sore myths
self-serving on mirrored haunches, bent
to receive their own flesh grown in a
   tested, pregnant pause

Crawling into the furled aviary, tucking
heads in their elbows
into the lead vaults
              whose suppositories
leach a trickle of Bertha & Anne & fast
hydrocarbons, tagged for peak blood-
plasma when disengagement has topped
a cradled & devising beast

Sprawled in dots of yellow on pools
   so clear they
hug Narcissus into their swelling plaits
   a break
about the limbs he strikes in
entering you reflected, shrunken Atlas

Israel, Horn of Africa on the news
or a spy satellite
   proud how your internal life
lent colour, shies off the unequivocal
with its slice in time
              O such brittle proofs
of the heart's heated topography
building the vault you invite yourself to

& where does the road now follow you
To the last reach of the semblable?
The like & the like
Dissolve inside that lead suit

Ice crackles like paper underfoot, & lifts
over the street & is carried off
Nightly the dreamers lay their skin out
down impassable roads
sealing the wounds & burns that obliterate
    cursive twists of the eye
But the ice overhead, a tracking sore
               is slicked on the negative
like a white lead elixir
        Hoarfrost grips their
brilliant bones, & their flickering eyes
shunt the wall of death for top compliance
  This way they paper the cracks
      they glide
  over the seam, they will lose
all grounds for semblance
                 Under the boot
white shadows are crushed to reveal wounds

Pull on to walk on face-masks of preterition, put the stamp
where suppliants of the order of your boot prepare for love
as for a funeral. Pull on to walk & kill & cure, belatedly
your stand-in stands in their cold blood beneath you. Slaves

not daring shake your image. Worn on a waist like a netsuke
Hung off an ear like a pendant. Walk where a thousand faces
shadow you in cold blood. No more can you cast your shadow
on ice than glass, no more shall you comb your slick tresses

to bravery. You beckon the stone, you will turn to a marble
vanity mirror, grave of shadows, lean out of the high tower
as if you might cast your proper self down. Reckon a crowd
from granite & into the white slab die the moon you supplant

Caught to the life, we contemplate in the sharpness of death
those like us. & ever the statue will move to our accents
biddable where the injurious light, where the patina floats
on an old sediment: ours is the mark at the lips of silence

caught to the life. Marble stains with the tears shed for it
Sperm spatters its thighs. A rose-tint colours the shoulder
we chafe reassuringly. Wrenching apart the torso, tearing
through the impacted layers of his presence, it is a corpse

with his oracle, into his mouth: it is his project for life
Here all resemblance ends in itself. Ghosts fan off his body
like cards from a shoe on the gaming table, ghosts of ivory
spill no blood, catching the careworn face which he loves

in their carrion light, now every dumb thing flocks for her
Underneath her lips still move. We who are husbands of death
slip through light with our acid tensity, we connoisseurs
who anchor the torso in an image, oracle of its own silence

Bear with me till the story breaks, till we look back over
honeyed paths of celluloid, unreeled as we fly out of Hades
Bear with me when I tell tales. If you touch I drop unpitied
into the net, a pouching seine already reasons against me

Light shines from a basement window, so does a fretful tower
shine the light. Lightrays quiver, light curtails my veins
I sit by a leaky stump. Polish them off with fair unbothered
not-face, don't permit the fingers to stop, or finger one

querulous flute. Then act the fool. Act as if I could catch
my fugitives, grinning & stamping my foot. When the stump
& the taper are leaking the gas of the hours & wearing off
I must immediately set to work. Bear me out to that good end

Yet you disperse like a swarm of bees. What shall I reembody
amidst the lamps? in their criminal origin, in the denial
we map through their long shots only, but cannot conceive
a black swarm behind them shadows & flaunts our familiarity

So much extravagance. O this extravagance never shall vary
in flights of absurdity, gospel truths, all fly to resort
where the sagging & mortal fool, the mortal of film collects
his auguries always delayed & misplaced, what we somewhere

now became. Hanging loose at the bottom of night's uncancel
This nostalgia calls me as I settle to work, & when I chivvy
its moths. But I bear & deliver my fugitives. Bear what I
distantly cannot. We answer our excuses & set out the lamps

Office-bound, the bored despot fingerpads her quilted hours
testing for give; *sostenuto* clicks the chorus of her bobbins
The sky elate & bitterly cold, halts fittingly, a backcloth:
roads settle in their aggregate, windows lift at the edge

& crinkle to a crease against the light that dries our pelts
curing them, once her incisiveness blocks them over cages
One casts his shadow to walk to his institute, how each is
flat & staid! An image makes the lover by whom it was meant

but what Pygmalion peaks for her eyes crawling over the cage
its shadow left, perusing on its lamp-black, keen to invent
her aboriginal tusk? She strokes her eye, she is finished
Depth she's already franchised out to sweet quilted fingers

Unity of consciousness stays open & shut at the box-bridge
Here the mists interfuse, provided its arches are calloused
with false destiny, where what but an echo crosses an echo
about my skull in rumours. A longitudinal slice of the brain

will show two lovers fade in porcelain light to chinoiserie
that as false origin indurates. They pass through each other
self-ravished, ghosts of a bridechamber, still they embrace
intentionally, & if the bridge they support seems perilous

of itself, it only is correct assumption. Yes a boot goes in
Yes I am in hospital, my jaw has been wired at full stretch
like a bridge the pulleys & ropes direct. Lead weights hang
from machinery far & indirect, & my boot stays in my mouth

Through stone, fossils are set. In the leafed ice, are chips
of turquoise. None of which bears a relation to that bridge
that I know of, unless it be one of identity. The harshest
lesson lies in a bridge letting any fracture run to be sure

Here he cages boots
behind the rough slats
polishing them up well
before he lets them out

He's so very tolerant
a child would say stupid
as he polishes a boot
he willingly will let go

Defenders run amok, tear past him, down the half-lit arcade
behind the lead glass, a concourse of energy; ache to clench
the mandible his clumsy mitts had turned, touch real life
& to sponsor this awakening, this odd bag of behaviours

where were the rest thrown. Where did they hoard the fleshy
rinds peeled off those hard nuts. O Telamon. Pelisse of snow
was flung for decency on chock-full traps; & at sub-zero
the torn liver, your furrowed pelt, the shanks make no mess

Then you can spell your body like a planchette, tapping out
the ideal organ wanted & laid on your counter. You reinvent
a cavity from hand & brain & the sexual bits, & a lack of
social skills is remedied. Scrape off the snowy trap old son

Go back now with no memory. These are your arms, transparent
too, & visible for the first time. A tongue to catch flies
Eyes pitched up to the dura mater. Since you were loved, so
you gain advantage. Will shrivels as tardive dyskinesia

Like a hub-band we take our grip. With backs knit painfully
as they bend to the wheel, with wills bent to excruciate
the swollen, splitting nave. Moss sucks our sweat as we fall
receding into the present; & what is this company we keep?

The cartel, the writ that runs the sequences, for *this one*—
this one fires the dendrites, the axle-tree, this one does
not register the first trace, the first cut was the weakest
When the tube goes dead; who are these mirrored but strange?

digging our graves, turning our peat at the abstract grin
we scraped against? Cut against our nerve. & leaning, strain
despondently on the mountainslope, till we see them lodged
where our choice had fallen already, on that haunch of our

antique shade. Thongs of muscle bind them. Dropping in neat
sclerosis, hub-caps & their bodywork strewn on the ridge
of stone, in puerperal seizure. Are they our representatives
behind the screen of cloud we hastily drew over the hills?

Exalted but so useless! But we totter & roll & we process
close on their tail, rapt in the view & more stony, crunched
by the rim we harden inside like foetuses. Scrapyard din
booms from slope to slope & we love the old casts it leaves

Now race towards the apocalyptic hush
    plaster saints the ill wind wets
that crumble into heaps of kaolin
Bury your head in the vault, but it bumps
    against real girders
This I regard as a slap in the face!
My hands are cut, & the spirochaete
circulates on the bland wind!
The living-room has a heap of snow
on its well-worn carpet, spikes of grass
    which are tremor-sensitive!
& the step you scruple, detonates
a mass grave, the ghosts will tumble out!
Each shadow with one lip of flesh
or a barbarous organ, each one
real where your step has crushed it!

Better to draw a veil. In snow I'm blissful with your secret
milk, all those body fluids that dribble & ooze & freeze
Best fold the creases. Ghosts of otherness rise for escorts
near to your hard, tight mouth. They get the better of us

always. Yet your smell! I dream it & the earth consolidates!
Catch it, rub my nose in it! Only to thinly spread myself
like snow on the asphalt, salt on snow, or snow on brine
Well may ghosts shiver & flurry, their drifting forms elide

Waking I found I knew so much, but nothing here would comply
Treetops high on the moor stake out their veil but float
in freezing fog, & the very air seems live with the powders
which as they touch me where I walk wet my hair & clothes

This morning will they include us, shattered & down at heel
kerb-anxious, chatting squalidly? We look to be compliant
as packed ice, dreaming into marble. How can I hold firm
bedraggled with specks of memory, with cold beads of desire?

Little calves
spindle with glee
silk-bran-scarfed
stiff-kneed

gorged on stuff
like a watermelon
watered
till fresh blood

swells indignantly
blurts the hide

Skew-whiff
the bondsman lures himself
through blood to a cool heart

each of his guests
touched at some extremity, *stuff*

where it grazes a passing abstract

Quietness
scabs on that infarction, LVF
floods & silences the chamber
So memory's excess
stumbles, like the whispering
gallery reduced to hard clitter

Moss upholsters skeletons

A controlled blast
rocks the deep-plush room

& the false viscera tremble

Knee-deep in the endocrine
Thick
in the surface view

live as a hair shirt

So we shall outlove

Unconscious grace that I caught as a gesture
repeated across the night, a tone-row
squashed into a pulse I time myself by

parades among the distorts in her azure coat
self-possessed; could it have thought to
pluck me like a seedling from a low box

of the things she isn't! lift from the swell
my heart had enrolled to the heart with
so to be buried close by steady shock

& feel I made gains on it, than should o she
resolved in the shadows, in foliage
smitten with blue faith, tear the earth

where my heart lay unpieced below its tumuli
of night-resemblance, wanting change
wanting to face a music she scores

with no harmonic development, no melodies to
follow to some throttled stop: this is
time which doesn't owe dues to the upright

but tacks against the ordinary line for such
an earnest & ardour, that her head-
tilt I was attached to, had to rip off

used to read her in each face! can emblemize
any world's look, from the susurrus
of dying empire to the sun's blue blaze

to what analogy she might tempt from the air
about her. Thus the original stands
for nothing, stands as the non-sequitur

of grace conforming transience to its figure

Mad for a little phrase, I've sought to cure
love through its impossible kind, kind
pain would assuage the scattered pain

till spaced out & delirious with its shy joy
it vaulted heaven-sent; how did a sour
cream of disillusion, lies come to smooth

my path one step ahead, why the false arcana
wherein love is reproduced? The cupole
fixed my eyes, I am a charlatan, a seer

attempting to ford the same difference, gulf
of my same affirmed denial. What I
never want, I learnt to want it, trading

parts like a Narcissistic Christ; open doors
paradisial, o clapped on hearts aplenty
hung to jackknife while a dead-sea-

apple cranes a dead mouth, swing to a common
dream they take their stock of, dyes
for every dazed trompe l'oeil. Who saved

the world in 1963? & who is the illegitimate
son of the pope? who moved steamboats
up the hill on rolls of coolies & cash?

Frightful cruelty moors its dome of paradise
over the pre-fab, smearing pigments
drawn from the cut veins of a disclosed

primitive in our eyes. It is the part-object
freaked with shadow & trading our body-
bits at a loss. Its huge curve amplifies

these to a solid whole when most specialized

Ramped on my surging throat, at full stretch
acting as the commensals to the spirit
guide which is a mole on your white back:

how we get whole is what diminishes us, what
shrivelled us to a nub, tiny buttons
complicate the emissaries so star-struck

we took ourselves as read; the already-eaten
come to our lips & the lipstick tags
its piece for a fetish, restrain yourself

now & always, otherwise I must eat my flesh:
you unwittingly fail, I hunch my throat
over its cud, on a chewed & deceitful

thing I applied my lip to. What might I love
if the earliest one to wear a black cap
shook & strummed & was near-undeniable?

blaring that silence bred in the firmament's
tight space? Systems pour from the gash
illimitably, yet caught in my throat

an insistent note harps like a life sentence
Was it for this the distressed heart
shook down to its makeshift, burst

in technicolour chromatics? Broke to observe
their awful resonance gain with a cheap
grandeur? Can this be how we inflate

our meaning presence from our demeaned lives
caressing the part-payments? Fetishists
at once & parasites, feasting to the stars

traumatic colour. Turning our backs for love

She assimilates all comparison into her like
no-one can seize for a limb; & the milky
way of the colonies has to turn far short

& seep in the nimbus of blue & deteriorating
photo-cells, that starve for the limited
blush of time a comparison would carry

What choice remains for us then but amputate
the nimbus, the diseased limb, how else
our sugars were to imagine or to repine

after the battered torso we'd long conceived
recombinant; pig-ignorant we fly to work
to fail before her, fleet & sound of limb

incorporating music while her ears are waxed
against a suitors' leaning rock we cleave
from clouds of *so like her*, the fontanel

we could neither hear nor watch nor mutilate
Fatigued by this we dabble in chance
over the foil, scraping free the pounce

disguising ranks of symbols of such aridness
they seem lush, choking earth with eager
compacts for renewal, grist for gangrene:

the readier we are the more we seek the same
atonement, suitable when the shorthand
of the admonished things, these our pranks

frequent her like witnesses, o intense inane
they jostle, even the stars are like stops
that shearing a torso out of fierce love

colonize its phantom limbs to prove her body

Armorial glass which sags in its leaden web
& the armoured, frosting into the sight
of its painstaker, blow & gape like sails

in the air I was adopted by, like parchment
beating & flapping over a choppy breath
What I blazon shall restore me & protect

with a patience born of indomitable display
or coil forlornly, waiting for a tutelary
whose warmth shall seal a living emblem

in blind alleys paved in hot & gentle stone
When the last crack is sutured, when she
calls to action the devices that I bear

will arms break against the day in lozenges
—Between my ruined figments & the shards
of a facing world, whose soggy pupa sits

if apostrophes concur in the meaning flesh?

The infant scream subsides
into a cancelled mutter:
o I am no more than a lax spring
explaining out its function

like a diseased heart
will analyze its reckless salvo
slavishly to the echo
crammed with standing waves

Racing, when the sure
& loved distance closes on it
presages in smell, of white
abandon to the last flutter

". . . and poignant is Cassiodorus' narrative of sacked Rome, populated by 5,000 men and 100,000 ideal marble figures."

Proud flesh: "Overgrown flesh arising from excessive granulation upon, or around the edges of, a healing wound." (SOED)

Index of first lines

& every soul forgive me, for I am self-forgiving	49
A fat photograph	17
Armorial glass which sags in its leaden web	78
As flickerbooks of the blistered but perennial ice	27
Away from scavengers who scuff & pry the weary peat	35
Bear with me till the story breaks, till we look back over	57
Better to draw a veil. In snow I'm blissful with your secret	64
Breaker one-nine	25
But ours is another ploy for power amidst blueberry hills	14
Caught to the life, we contemplate in the sharpness of death	56
Chaff or husk or bran the dark has held fritters away	30
Clay when the wire slackens, sheds its velvet light	6
Cloud-blue affliction skims & trails his antibodies	22
Contracts	44
Darkness, thickly feathered, squats to eat, the lucid	16
Deceitful as the first breach in the sense-world	48
Defenders run amok, tear past him, down the half-lit arcade	61
Distraught with its self-aggrandisement, the brain-	37
Does snow or polystyrene, crisp the noise he went after	28
Doors open to the metal crash of insects, & outside	9
Every metaphor sounds the same	5
For years this had been a waking hurt. Dear violence	36
Geomancers pick among these trinkets in their play-pen	15
Ghosts walk through you as much by day	52
He smears	8
Here he cages boots	60
I pulled it out of my lungs	41
Ice & dead skin	42
Ice crackles like paper underfoot, & lifts	54
In the losing light, see, your head	10
In this trial run for behaviour, sculling then as now, a dry run	43
Jealously given a cup, filled with a black aperitif	39
Knee-deep in the endocrine	69
Like a hub-band we take our grip. With backs knit painfully	62
Little calves	65

Lorraine will cruise	23
Love compels me to its dialect, love whose law	34
Love is brought to fulfilment by this art, distributed	29
Mad for a little phrase, I've sought to cure	72
Moss upholsters skeletons	68
Moths feed at this window, bury their drear heads in light	19
Narrowly in the kitchen, coffee brews	51
Now race towards the apocalyptic hush	63
Nurselings of a pitched eye visit the grey stalk	47
O where is the breast I left part of my mouth on?	50
Office-bound, the bored despot fingerpads her quilted hours	58
Or is it Crab-boy	24
Pavements I walk	13
Pull on to walk on face-masks of preterition, put the stamp	55
Quietness	67
Ramped on my surging throat, at full stretch	74
She assimilates all comparison into her like	76
Skew-whiff	66
Slender pickings fall to the lap of the foster-child	3
Snap out of it then! Pull yourself together at once!	40
Strip the caul from my face, fold it & bury it fast	38
The infant scream subsides	79
The key that fastens the door turns any lock in my body	21
They bash their fists on the asphalt playground, as if	4
Unconscious grace that I caught as a gesture	70
Underfoot	31
Unity of consciousness stays open & shut at the box-bridge	59
Waste breath drifts. Breath condenses	32
We'd launch out, but a spiral failure binds so close	7
Where light slashes I'll break into flower. Does brocade	12
Will the man in the moon blink in his stuffy globe?	26
X marks your hinterness	18
Your words catch in the throat that I gulp & incessantly	20

Printed in the United Kingdom
by Lightning Source UK Ltd.
106991UKS00001B/28-36